The
Secret
Message

The Secret Message

Idella Bodie

SANDLAPPER PUBLISHING CO., INC.
ORANGEBURG, SOUTH CAROLINA 29115

Published by Sandlapper Publishing Co., Inc.
Orangeburg, South Carolina 29115

First Edition

Book design by Barbara Stone
Manufactured in the United States of America

Library of Congress Cataloging-in-Publication Data

Bodie, Idella
   The secret message / Idella Bodie. — 1st ed.
     p.   cm. — (Heroes and heroines of the American Revolution)
     Includes bibliographical references (p.   ).
     Summary: The story of Emily Geiger, a young heroine of the
American Revolution who crossed through enemy territory to deliver
a message from General Greene to General Sumter.
     ISBN 0-8744-145-X
     1. Geiger, Emily, b. 1762 or 3—Juvenile literature. 2. Women
heroes—South Carolina—Biography—Juvenile literature. 3. Teenage
girls—South Carolina—Biography—Juvenile literature. 4. United
States—History—Revolution, 1775–1783—Women—Juvenile
Literature. 5. South Carolina—History—Revolution, 1775–1783—
Women—Juvenile literature. 6. Greene, Nathanael, 1742–1786—
Juvenile literature.   [1. Geiger, Emily, b. 1762 or 3. 2. Heroes.
3. Teenage girls—Biography. 4. Women—Biography. 5. United
States—History—Revolution, 1775–1783. 6. South Carolina—
History—Revolution, 1775–1783. 7. Greene, Nathanael, 1742–1786.]
I. Title. II. Series.
E263.S7B64   1998
973.7'092—dc21
[B]   98-6715
                                            CIP
                                            AC

South Carolina's
Most Exciting Heroine
of the Revolutionary War

In the summer of 1781 General Nathanael Greene, commander of the American Continental Army in the South, needed to get a message to General Thomas Sumter. Unfortunately, British Lord Francis Rawdon and his large army lay between Greene's and Sumter's camps. What was General Greene to do?

Emily Geiger, a farmer's daughter, came to his aid.

~*ACKNOWLEDGEMENTS*~

I wish to express my appreciation to the staff of the Cayce Museum for the use of their outstanding research on Emily Geiger: to Rachel Worthy Steen for gathering the material for me and to historian Clayton Kleckley who read my manuscript for accuracy.

To the Young Reader

During the Revolutionary War many women found themselves surrounded by conflict. Sadly, almost all of their contributions to the cause were not recorded.

Women cared for their families, nursed wounded soldiers, worked in fields, tended farm animals, and performed many other tasks. While they were engaged in these duties, they often heard news of enemy movements in the area. Some took long rides into Patriot camps to report what they had learned. Young women also showed courage and loyalty to the American cause. Emily Geiger was bold enough to take a message from General Nathanael Greene to General Thomas Sumter.

Emily Geiger was born about 1760 in the Up Country of South Carolina. Her father, John Geiger, was a planter. Mr. Geiger's health and age kept him from bearing arms for his country, but he was a devoted Patriot. When Emily heard that General Greene had a desperate need to get a message to General Sumter many miles away, she volunteered to be the messenger.

Since no written account was made at the time of Emily's ride, some people think of her heroic deed as legend. Yet today's records show Emily was a real person who did indeed take a dangerous ride through enemy territory to deliver a message.

For many years this teenager's daring deed was told over and over by those who knew her. Because the event was not recorded until decades later, accounts differ in sequence of events and places. Of course it is impossible to repeat with authority conversations that took place so long ago. However, for reader interest I have dramatized scenes as facts lead us to believe they happened.

Contents

The
Secret
Message

1.
Greene's Camp

Maybinton, South Carolina

June 1781

General Nathanael Greene paced back and forth in the hot quarters of his tent, pitched on the western bank of Broad River. His stiff knee didn't seem to work right this morning, but that was not his real problem.

"If only I could get a message to Sumter at his camp on Wateree River." The general spoke more to himself than to his aide. "With Rawdon's troops marching toward the Low Country, we could band together and defeat him. But alone—" Greene shook his head and continued pacing.

"Your men know the problem, Sir," his aide said. "Have you no volunteers?"

"None. And I can't say that I blame them. The land between our camps is thick with Tories. A lone rider in a Continental uniform wouldn't stand a chance of getting through."

"You are right, Sir. And the Tories are showing no mercy. It would be a useless death."

"Besides, my men who survived the battle at Ninety Six are worn out. Many suffer wounds." Greene stopped pacing and stroked his brow in worry. "I will not order a man to his death."

Once again he picked up the pacing. *What was he to do?*

2.
Emily's Decision
Maybinton, South Carolina

In a farmhouse a short distance away, Emily Geiger tossed in her bed. She would never get to sleep after what she had overheard earlier in the evening.

She was used to hearing talk of battle. It wasn't that. The Revolutionary War had been going on around her for more than five years. And, she had learned to be careful of what she said, especially in front of her Tory neighbors.

It was the news a

Patriot friend had brought her father that bothered her. "Lord Rawdon has abandoned Star Fort at Ninety Six," he said. "Right now he is marching his troops toward the coast, and I hear he's coming by Granby."

"Why, that will cut off General Greene's communication to the rest of his army," her father replied. "I hear Sumter's camped on Wateree River."

"That's the problem." The visitor's voice was just above a whisper, and Emily had to raise her head from her pillow to hear. "Greene knows he could never get a message past all the Tories *and* their spies."

Emily knew her father didn't like her listening in on adult conversations, but she couldn't help herself. According to the visitor's directions, a messenger would need to travel the very route she took on visits to Cousin Elizabeth.

Emily sat up straight in her bed. It was a long way, but she knew Congaree Swamp like the back of her hand.

Suddenly she stopped breathing. Would General Greene and her father allow her to take the message? She let out a heavy sigh. Both men thought women had no place in war.

For a while Emily sat deep in thought. Then she folded her arms across her chest. She had made a decision. *She would do it! No one would suspect a girl.*

"They will have to listen to me," she told herself. "They have no other choice."

Her mind made up, Emily lay back down. In the morning she would ride her horse the short distance to General Greene's camp.

3.
Emily's Request

Greene's Camp

The following morning a guard appeared at the opening of General Greene's tent.

"Excuse me, Sir," he said, "but a young lady is here to see you."

Greene turned. His worried expression became one of puzzlement.

"A young lady?" Emily heard him ask. "What would a woman

be doing here?"

"Sir, she said something about delivering a message."

"Send her in."

In moments, Emily was in the tent curtsying before the general. She could feel her heart pounding beneath her dark riding habit. She fidgeted with her small riding whip.

Finally, Emily found the nerve to face the general. She felt her face flush as she spoke. "I have heard, General, that you need someone to take a message to General Sumter."

"That is true," the general replied, still puzzled. "As yet," he went on," I have found no one bold enough to undertake the mission."

"Then send me!" Emily's voice rang with excitement.

"Send *you*? Why, I could not do that, my child! It is a journey from which brave men hold back. And your father?"

"He loves his country, Sir, and he feels the same way you do about a woman's place." She began to speak faster. "But even if he doesn't want me to go, he won't stop me."

"How old are you, my dear?"

"Eighteen, Sir."

"What is your name, Child?"

"Emily Geiger, Sir."

Greene began to pace again. He thought more clearly when he moved about.

"I have a fleet horse, Sir." Emily felt her eagerness rising. "I know the way, and I can bear your message."

For a while all was quiet. Finally, Greene stopped pacing.

"Noble girl, you are right. No one would suspect you of carrying a message. Meet me here in the morning."

4.
Off with the Message

The following morning Emily stood before General Greene to receive instructions.

"Before you go," the general said, "read this dispatch." He handed her a parchment with a message written in black ink.

Emily bowed her head over the firm handwriting. Her eyes sped over Greene's dispatch to Sumter.

When she turned her bright face toward the general, he took the paper, folded it, and once again held it out to her.

Emily quickly hid the note in the folds of her bodice.

"If you are arrested," General Greene said, "destroy the message as quickly as you can." Then he grasped her hand. "God speed and protect you. May heaven and your country reward you."

Word of Emily's mission had spread through the camp, and soldiers gathered to see her off. One soldier cupped his palms for Emily's boot to help her mount sidesaddle.

With "God bless you!" ringing in her ears, she dug her heel in her horse's side and galloped away.

Courtesy of South Caroliniana Library, University of South Carolina, Columbia

5.
A Lonely Ride

Emily tried to calm her heart as she traveled the long, lonely stretch of land bordering Broad River.

"I must pretend I am only going to Uncle Jacob's for a visit," she told herself. "I will not be afraid."

Urging her horse on, she imagined how happy Cousin Elizabeth would be to see her and what fun they would have catching up on what each had done since they were together.

Careful to stay hidden by woods, she rode on until late afternoon. She passed Morgan's

Range and took a path toward Saluda River. At Kennedy's Ferry she would cross the Saluda and follow Congaree River toward Sumter's camp.

The woods grew darker. Evening shadows fell about her. The house where she expected to stay for the night was still miles away. Her horse needed rest. She was tired too. She would stop at the next farmhouse she saw.

Before long, Emily stood facing a cabin door. A kind man asked where she was headed.

When Emily gave her relatives' name, he answered, "Why, that's over ten miles. You'd better stay with us."

The man led Emily's horse to the stable while his wife invited her for supper.

"Have you come far?" the woman asked. "Your horse looked tired."

Emily hesitated. She did not know these people. Was she with friends?

"I rode fast," she answered.

"It's not safe for you to ride alone in these times," the woman said. "Surely you've heard that General Greene has retreated from Ninety Six. I'm sure some of his ragamuffins are about."

Emily felt a sudden chill. *This family was on the side of the Tories!*

6.
A Narrow Escape

The Tory woman stared at Emily. "What is your name?" she asked.

Again Emily hesitated before she replied, "Emily Geiger."

"Not John Geiger's daughter!"

Emily nodded. "Yes," she said in a weak voice.

The woman turned to her husband who was entering the room. "Can you believe it? This girl is the daughter of John Geiger we have heard so much about."

Emily's thoughts churned. What was she to do? If she left now, she would surely look suspicious.

"No wonder your horse is so tired," she heard the man saying. "If you've ridden that far, no doubt you are hungry too."

He put up his hand to the questioning look on his wife's face. "Let's have supper. She should have food and shelter even if she is the daughter of our enemy."

After the meal, the woman showed Emily to her room.

Alone, Emily wondered what she should do. But before she could decide, she had fallen into a deep sleep.

Sometime in the night she was awakened by the sound of horses' hoofs.

A voice called out, "Hello in there Preston! I may be on a fool's errand, but have you seen a stray woman in these parts?"

Emily's blood turned cold. *A Tory spy was looking for her!*

The shutters of Emily's window were open to the night air. She eased up to see a rider dismount and enter the house. For a long time she heard voices murmuring. Then all was quiet.

"They must be waiting until morning to

capture me," Emily thought. "I have to get away."

Moving as quietly as she could, Emily escaped through her window and into the moonlight. In the stable she searched for her horse. She located a bridle but not her saddle. Hurriedly she mounted and sped off.

Near daylight Emily reached the home where she had planned to stay and poured out her story. The Patriot friends gave her a fresh horse. Just as the sun rose, she swept away once more on her mission.

7.
Captured

By evening of the second day Emily rode along the edge of a dried swamp, making her way to Friday's Ferry on Congaree River. Suddenly her heart leaped. Three Tory soldiers rode in her direction. They had seen her. It would be no use to turn back.

As tired as she was, Emily tried to sit tall. She must act brave.

Before she knew what was happening, the soldiers were upon her. The one in front dismounted and grabbed her horse's bridle. In his other hand he held a musket. A second jumped from his horse and dropped down in

a crouching position with his rifle. The third also dismounted and leaned against a tree as if waiting to see what would happen.

The soldier holding her bridle spoke first. "Why, pray tell, is a young woman like you out riding alone through country like this?" he asked.

"I'm on my way to visit relatives." Emily

tried hard to keep her voice from shaking.

The soldier leaning against the tree stepped forward. "I don't think so," he said. "I believe she is on a secret mission."

Emily took a deep breath. "If you think I am here for any other reason than the one I have told you, then fetch a matron to search me."

The soldiers looked at each other. What were they thinking? The one holding Emily's bridle began to lead her horse toward his own. Another grabbed her satchel. *She was their prisoner!*

The four traveled under tall pines, cypress, and oaks that Emily knew so well. But never before had she taken a ride like this.

"I must not panic," she kept telling

herself. "I will think of something. I have to, not only for my sake but for my country's."

A distance away Emily found herself locked in an upstairs room of a farmhouse, one the British had taken over and made into a fort. They called it Fort Granby.

She knew without a doubt the soldiers were sending for a Tory matron to search her. *What was she to do?*

8.
Searched

Emily's mind raced. She had to do something fast. She slipped the note from her bodice and looked about. It would be foolish to try to hide it. With trembling hands she unfolded the parchment and read it again as she had in General Greene's tent.

The words burned themselves into her memory. She closed her eyes and repeated the message word for word. Suddenly she had an idea.

She frantically ripped the tough parchment into shreds. With the pieces as small as she could make them, she started

Courtesy of South Caroliniana Library, University of South Carolina, Columbia

stuffing them into her mouth. The paper was so dry it almost choked her, but she managed to chew and swallow every trace.

When the Tory matron entered the room, no sign of a message could be found.

Embarrassed over finding nothing against Emily, the soldiers offered an apology. They even sent her under escort to her cousin's home where she spent the night.

The next morning when Emily rode out to continue her journey, she did not go the direct route to General Sumter's camp. Instead, she followed an old Indian trail pointed out by her relatives.

Finally, she crossed Friday's Ferry and headed toward Sumter's camp on Wateree River.

In late afternoon, faint, weary, and sick with hunger, Emily saw the tent rows of the Patriot camp.

Drawing her horse's reins before the guard, she said in a weak voice, "Take me to General Sumter. I have a message from

General Greene."

Soon Emily stood before the general and repeated word for word the contents of the dispatch she had destroyed.

General Sumter never doubted Emily's word. He gave an immediate command. Shortly, the camp's band gathered. Drums rattled and clarions blew. Their march was on.

9.
Honors for the
Teenage Heroine

After the Revolutionary War ended, Emily married John Threrwitz, a planter. They lived near Granby, South Carolina, which is now Cayce. Emily died shortly after giving birth to her first child, Elizabeth Juliet, who lived to be only five years old.

Records disagree about the date of Emily's death. Some give 1783 as the year, yet a copy of her wedding invitation in the Cayce Museum is dated 1789. The Geiger family history simply says Emily died in the 1780s.

Though many gravestones are worn and parts are missing, it is believed Emily's grave lies in the Threrwitz family cemetery on Old Charleston Highway (U. S. 176) in the Dixiana community of Lexington County. In 1926 a chapter of the Daughters of the American Revolution unveiled a marker to Emily in the cemetery. A memorial also stands in her honor in the Geiger family cemetery just a few miles away in the community of Sandy Run.

Cherry Laurel, Emily's home after marriage, still stands near Silver Lake in Dixiana.

It is said that General Greene visited Emily in 1783 and presented her a set of jewelry and a silver pencil.

South Carolina has honored Emily Geiger

for her contribution to freedom with a plaque in the State House. When the State seal was redesigned after the victory on Sullivan's Island, an image of a woman holding a branch of laurel was added. It was later suggested that the woman, representing hope overcoming dangers, be designated as Emily Geiger because of her bravery during the Revolutionary War.

Most importantly, the story of a teenager who volunteered for a dangerous assignment continues to be told after all these years.

Words Needed for Understanding

bodice	that part of a dress worn above the waist
clarions	trumpets
Continental	relating to a soldier of the American colonies during the American Revolution
curtsy	bending the knees and lowering the body in respect; a type of bow offered by women to figures of honor (used in America only prior to twentieth century; used today with royalty in some European countries)
dispatch	a message sent quickly
fetch	go after and bring back a person or thing
ferry	a flat boat used for carrying people, animals, goods, etc., across a river
fidgeted	moved nervously

matron	an older, mature woman
musket	a long-barreled firearm
paced	walked back and forth
panic	a fear that seems hard to handle; a sudden fear
parchment	paper made from animal skin or material that has the appearance of skin
puzzlement	a look of not understanding; bewilderment
ragamuffin	a dirty, ragged person
riding habit	clothing worn by a rider of a saddle horse
satchel	a small bag for carrying clothes, etc.
Tory	a person living in the colonies who gave allegiance to the King of England during the American Revolution

Things to Do and Talk About

1. Draw a map of South Carolina. Put in the major rivers and cities. Locate the major battlegrounds of the Revolutionary War and add them to your map. Trace Emily Geiger's ride. Add your hometown and study the location of your sites.

2. Accounts of Emily's ride vary as to how many days she traveled. Several accounts give the distance as over 100 miles. Using a South Carolina map that lists mileage, how long do you think it would have taken her?

3. Make quick comparison of how different General Greene's communication would be today.

4. Study the South Carolina seal. Can you explain how the design on it relates to our country's struggle for freedom? The woman on the seal appears to walk along a shoreline strewn with sword daggers. In her hand she holds a laurel branch. Can you relate these symbols to Emily Geiger's heroic deed?

5. Research some long-ago happening you've heard about in your area. See if you find conflicting records on dates and places. Why do you think this might have happened? Can you decide which must be right? What did you base that decision on? Can you understand how such mistakes could have occurred?

6. Has your family name always had the same spelling it now has? Emily's married name was Threrwitz, but it was also spelled Threewits, Threewitts, and Thruwitts. My married name once had two *d*s: Boddie.

7. Do you know of a person in the twentieth century who did a heroic deed for his/her country? Write about this person or make an oral report to your class. Explain why his/her deed is considered heroic.

8. Do you think it would seem as unusual today for a woman to volunteer for such a dangerous mission? Explain your views. Support your opinion with an example from today's world.

9. Form small groups in your classroom and

write plays based on the chapters in this book. Besides writers, actors, and actresses, you will need stage directors, as well as set and costume designers. Perform your play before other classes.

10. If distance permits, visit the Cayce Historical Museum at 1800 Twelfth Street Extension in Cayce. Be sure to call ahead for reservations: 803-796-9020, ext. 3030.

Sources Used

Archives of Cayce Museum, including articles on the papers of Dr. Lyman C. Draper by historian Lee R. Gandee and affidavits by John Threewits Nicholson (September 9, 1922) and Harriet McCollough Legare (February 3, 1931), relatives of Emily Geiger, providing proof of Emily's existence and of her heroic ride during the American Revolution.

Claghorn, Charles E. *Women Patriots of the American Revolution.* Metuchen, NJ: Scarecrow Press, 1991.

Ellet, Elizabeth F. *Women of the Revolution.* Vol. 2. New York: Haskell House Publishers, 1969.

"Emily Geiger: A Heroine of the Revolution." *American Monthly Magazine*, vol. 8 (March 1896).

Farley, M. Foster. *Newberry County in the American Revolution.* Newberry, SC: County Bicentennial Committee, 1975.

Hilborn, Nat, and Sam Hilborn. *Battleground of Freedom.* Columbia, SC: Sandlapper Press, 1970.

Means, Celina E. *Palmetto Stories*. New York: Macmillan, 1983.

Ripley, Warren. *Battleground: South Carolina in the Revolution*. Charleston, SC: Evening Post Publishing Company, 1983.

Shealy, W. A. "Emily Geiger, A True Story of the Revolution." *The Illustrator* (September 1896).

~ ~ ~

About the Author

IDELLA BODIE was born in Ridge Spring, South Carolina, and has always lived in this state. She holds a degree in English from Columbia College and for many years taught high school English and creative writing. Each year she makes many visits to schools and libraries around the state.

Mrs. Bodie lives in Aiken with her husband Jim.

~ ~ ~

Check with your local library and bookstore for these books by Idella Bodie:

- **Carolina Girl:** *A Writer's Beginning*

  NONFICTION—AUTOBIOGRAPHY

  The author recollects her childhood on a South Carolina farm during the Great Depression and her coming-of-age during World War II.

  "Bodie looks back on her childhood . . . with nostalgic magic, recapturing a way of life that is so alien to today's youths that they surely will find it fascinating."—The State (Columbia, SC)

- **Ghost in the Capitol**

  FICTION—NOVEL

  Three friends attempt to *exorcise* a ghost from the South Carolina state capitol in Columbia.

  ". . . a frightening, fun-filled adventure."—Evening Post (Charleston, SC)

- **Ghost Tales for Retelling**

  FICTION—SHORT STORIES

  A selection of ghost tales recollected from the author's childhood.

  "Kids and parents alike will enjoy reading or hearing the scary yarns Bodie related so well."—The Pilot (Southern Pines, NC)

♣ A Hunt for Life's Extras:
The Story of Archibald Rutledge

NONFICTION—BIOGRAPHY

The story of South Carolina's first poet laureate.

"Rutledge was a unique South Carolinian—a combination outdoorsman, conservationist and man of letters. Bodie has captured his essence in a study which makes the reader wish for more."—Sun News (Myrtle Beach, SC)

♣ The Man Who Loved the Flag

NONFICTION—BIOGRAPHY, FROM THE SERIES, "HEROES AND HEROINES OF THE AMERICAN REVOLUTION"

The story of Sergeant William Jasper who risked his life to save the flag when Fort Moultrie was under attack by the British.

". . . a concise biography for elementary-school students of Sgt. William Jasper, one of South Carolina's Revolutionary War heroes. . . . Bodie writes a descriptive account about Jasper's life, highlighting his dedication to freedom and his country's flag."—Carologue (S. C. Historical Society)

♣ The Mystery of Edisto Island

FICTION—NOVEL

Four friends try to help a sea island fisherman in trouble and end up facing real danger.

"Bodie handles suspense especially well, and readers over the age of 9 will be turning pages frantically to find out what happens in the next chapter."—Georgia Guardian (Savannah, GA)

The Mystery of the Pirate's Treasure

FICTION—NOVEL

Two brothers visiting Charleston, South Carolina, share an adventure involving buried treasure and graveyards at midnight.

"... a most interesting mystery story for the 10 to 14 set."—*Aiken Standard* (Aiken, SC)

The Secret of Telfair Inn

FICTION—NOVEL

A brother and sister try to discover what old Mr. Crow is hiding in an unused part of a spooky hotel.

"... the mystery is intriguing, parts are shivery and the end is satisfying with all loose ends tied neatly."—*Herald-Journal* (Spartanburg, SC)

South Carolina Women

NONFICTION—BIOGRAPHY

Vignettes on women from South Carolina who have impacted state and/or national history.

"... an excellent addition to a home or school library."—*Sun News* (Myrtle Beach, SC)

Stranded!

FICTION—NOVEL

Young friends find real adventure on Lake Murray when they cross paths with an escaped convict.

"[Bodie] manages to create a story full of stirring action, and, at the same time, deals sensitively with the practical and moral aspects of capital punishment and loyalty to friends and parents."—*Citizen-News* (Asheville, NC)

Trouble at Star Fort

FICTION—NOVEL

Classmates on a weekend camping trip find that recreating a Revolutionary War battle in an old fort at midnight can be fun—and frightening.

"Fun and educational for preteens."—Sandlapper Magazine

Whopper

FICTION—NOVEL

Howie is bored in school and creates "whoppers" to entertain himself. Unfortunately, his friends and family don't appreciate the tall tales. A special school visitor teaches him a fun way to use his imagination and stay out of trouble.

". . . honest and engaging, but with no comments or episodes that would rob a child of his childhood."— Guideposts

NOTE TO TEACHERS:

An activities guide to *Trouble at Star Fort* and a creative writing guide to *Whopper* are available to teachers using these books in their classrooms. For information, call Sandlapper Publishing Co., Inc., 1-800-849-7263.

The
Secret
Message